TEN LANDSCAPES

TEN LANDSCAPES
SHUNMYO MASUNO

EDITED BY JAMES GRAYSON TRULOVE

Rockport Publishers, Inc.

Rockport, Massachusetts

editor in the fields of landscape architecture, art, graphic design, and architecture. He is publisher and co-founder of Spacemaker Press, an imprint specializing in books on landscape art and architecture. His most recent books are *The New American Garden* (Whitney, 1998) and *The New American Cottage* (Whitney, 1999). Trulove is a recipient of the Loeb Fellowship from Harvard University's Graduate School of Design. He resides in Washington, D.C.

First published in the United States of America by:

Rockport Publishers, Inc.
33 Commercial Street
Gloucester, Massachusetts 01930-5089
Telephone: (978) 282-9590
Facsimile: (978) 283-2742

Distributed to the book trade and art trade in the United States by:

North Light Books, an imprint of
F & W Publications
1507 Dana Avenue
Cincinnati, Ohio 45207
Telephone: (800) 289-0963

Other distribution by:

Rockport Publishers, Inc.
Gloucester, Massachusetts 01930-5089

ISBN 1-56496-614-3

10 9 8 7 6 5 4 3 2 1

Design: James Pittman
Cover Image: Minao Tabata

Printed in China.

CONTENTS

FOREWORD

by H.I.H. Prince Norihito Takamado

Japan is a small country, but it stretches in a long line of islands over 3,500 kilometers, and so it is blessed with a climate and terrain of astonishing variety-from northern areas where snowfall averages more than ten meters in winter, to tropical regions noted for pineapples, mangoes, and other lush vegetation. It is divided by a backbone of mountain ranges, covered by a variety of vegetation, and has many lakes, swift-flowing streams, and fertile plains well suited for cultivation. In addition, as it is completely surrounded by oceans, it enjoys both arctic and tropical currents, and is rich in myriad types of fish.

But Japan is especially blessed in having four distinct seasons, the shifting of which mark four clear accents in the lives of its people. At the same time, the subtle shift in the seasons has endowed the Japanese people with a fine sensitivity to almost imperceptible changes. The seasonal variation in Japan's plant life inspired not only the art of flower arrangement (ikebana), but also the sense of impermanence that was infused into the spirit of the tea ceremony (cha no yu), which, indeed, is the very basis of Zen Buddhism.

The daily lives of the Japanese were based on agriculture and fishing, both of which are intricately connected with the seasons. Thus, numerous festivals and customs are based upon and reflect the seasons. The wide seasonal variety and range of agricultural produce-both cultivated and wild-and the profusion of fresh fish available have fostered the gourmet concept that all foods should be consumed at precisely the peak (shun) of their season.

So it has come to pass that the Japanese have become intricately connected to the seasons and to nature. Thanks to a natural setting that is mild, rich in seasonal change, and blessed with the fruits of the mountains, fields, and seas, the Japanese were able to create a culture that coexisted in harmony with nature, in a spirit of gratitude for their blessings.

The Japanese have thus come to "infuse nature" into everything around them in their daily lives. And, even though it exists within nature, this is also true of the creation of a garden. In a Japanese garden, whether large or small, what is important is whether or not it "looks natural." It should remind the viewer that the boulders, rocks, trees, shrubs, or grasses were there long before there was any type of building or garden at all.

This is true not only of the interior of the garden, but even the surrounding views-for even the distant mountains seen far beyond the living hedge or wall surrounding the garden proper were brought in and used as integral parts of the garden. This is called "borrowed landscape" (shakkei)-it entails a subtle union of distant aspects of nature with one's own garden. Thus, it can be said that Japanese gardens are an expression of the creator's ability to be in harmony with nature, the world, and even the very universe.

Zen priest and garden designer Shunmyo Masuno believes that "the garden is a special spiritual place in which the mind dwells." The gardens he creates are thus special crystallizations that express the depths of his mind.

At present, Shunmyo serves as assistant priest under his father, Shinpo Masuno, the resident priest, at Kenkoh-ji temple in Yokohama, at which there is a "strolling" (kaiyu-shiki) garden. While strolling through this garden, one can see a number of scenes that are expressive of many events in the life of Sakyamuni Buddha. One of the things that led to Shunmyo's becoming a landscape architect was certainly his being born into a Zen family. Indeed, it is precisely because of his deep insight and philosophy as

The opening of the Canadian Museum of Civilization garden took place while I was on an official visit to Canada, and thus I was able to attend. The Japanese garden is located on the roof of the museum, and is named "Wakei no Niwa," and, as it had just been moistened by a light rain, it richly exuded a palpable Japanese sensibility.

The garden in Kohjimachi Kaikan is on the fourth floor. It is a small courtyard that is surrounded by rooms and corridors. In that narrow space, Shunmyo has created four different worlds that can be viewed from four different sides. Into the traditional design of a Japanese garden, he has successfully infused a modern breath of life.

I do not know to what extent those of you who read this book will be able to grasp the reality of the gardens from viewing the photographs, but if you could begin to glimpse what sort of dialogue Shunmyo Masuno had with the plants and stones, and what types of worlds he was attempting to create, I should be extremely pleased, because that work embodies the very spirit of Japan itself.

ABOVE: *Shunmyo at the gate in Kenkoh-ji temple.*

HOTEL KOHJIMACHI KAIKAN

The Garden of Blue Mountains and Green Water

There are few places in the city capable of reproducing the sublime effects of Nature. Stands of trees, pools and fountains, and flowerbeds surrounding buildings cannot truly duplicate the wild elements of the natural world. Sprawling urban centers may inspire awe, but they seldom offer a sense of peace or repose.

Hotel Kohjimachi Kaikan, in Chiyoda, Tokyo, is located in just such a harsh environment. It is surrounded by a garden designed to provide the casual visitor with a memorable moment of peace during a short visit. It is a Japanese garden, however, not nature itself. It is a spiritual space designed according to sophisticated Japanese aesthetic principles that evoke and celebrate nature. Such a garden truly is what is needed in the urban environment.

The Kohjimachi Kaikan was designed to contain several small internal garden spaces. They are laid out as terraces, one on the main floor and two on the fourth floor, providing a natural atmosphere for contemplation and revitalization in the chaotic heart of Tokyo. The gardens adhere to the traditional Japanese sense of beauty and the spirit of Zen, to which we applied a modern understanding. This garden would be classified as a work of the Heisei era.

The three small gardens are called Seizan-Ryokusui No Niwa (The Garden of Blue Mountains and Green Water). The vision they convey is one of absolute peacefulness, as if one were deep within the forested mountains.

The waterfall garden on the main floor mingles the peaceful, refreshing, and musical sounds of running water. Flowing water is symbolized through the use of gravel in the two gardens on the fourth floor, where the viewer may imagine a running river. This area totally separates the viewer from the urban environment. One is left to meditate in silence on the meaning of such a space, with its harmonic marriage of water and plants. The layering of tree branches and the composition of rocks further imply the endless extension of the space. In Zen this convergence of natural and manmade objects creates an experience that reveals the cosmos and is referred to yohaku, or blankness. It is a moment of opportunity that unites people with nature.

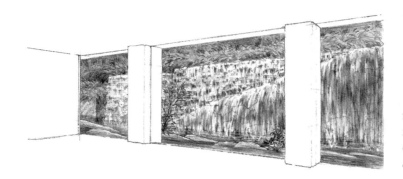

LEFT: *Sketch*
BELOW: *Plan on 1st floor*
OPPOSITE PAGE: *Night view of the cascade and pond*

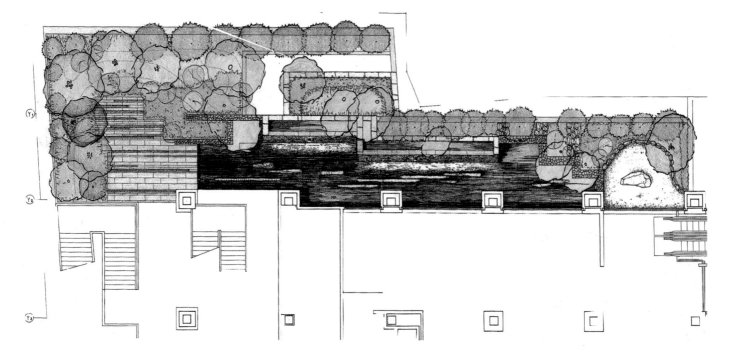

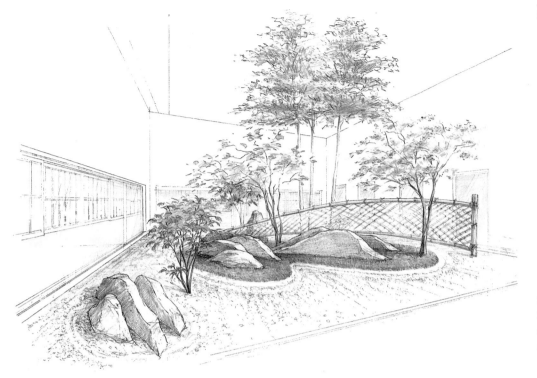

LEFT: *Sketch*
BELOW: *Plan on 4th floor*
OPPOSITE PAGE: *Rock arrangement and Kohetuji-style bamboo fence*

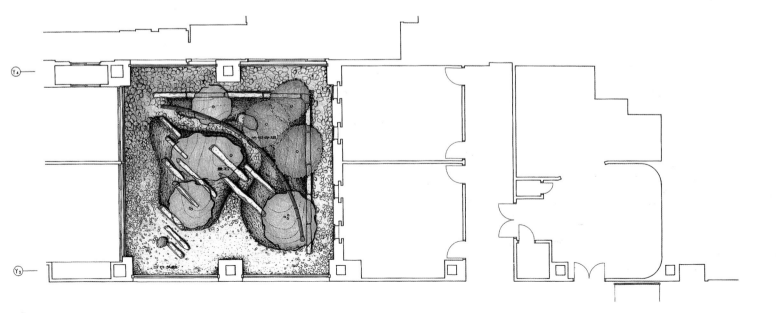

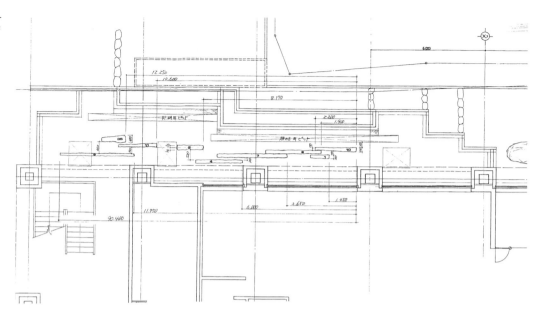

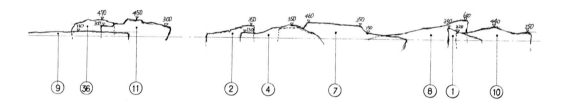

TOP: *Plan of waterfall and pond on the 1st floor*
MIDDLE: *Elevation for the layout of rocks*
BOTTOM: *Section for the layout of rocks*

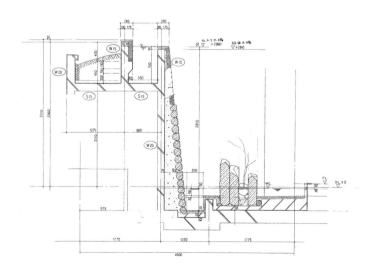

CLOCKWISE FROM UPPER LEFT: *Trial setting of rocks at Mure-machi; checking color harmony among different stones; marking a rock for fashioning; placed rocks and stone wall on 1st floor; checking the flow of cascade*

RIGHT: *Second Japanese garden on fourth floor*
BELOW: *Plan of garden on 4th floor*

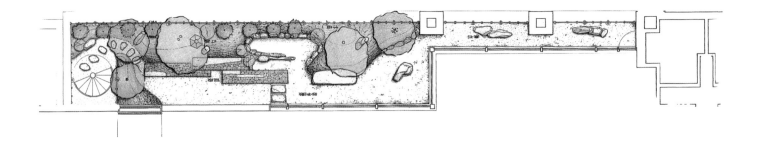

LEFT: *Bamboo fence hiding adjacent buildings*
BELOW LEFT: *Sketch*

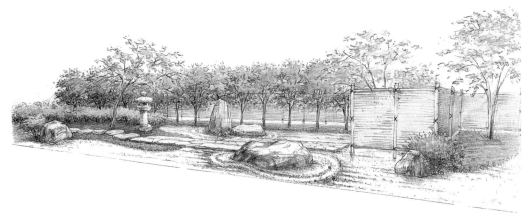

IMABARI KOKUSAI HOTEL

The Garden of a Great Waterfall and Pine Trees

This Japanese garden was inspired by the Setonaikai area in Japan, where Imabari is located. It consists of two distinct gardens. Water is the motif of the main garden, and simplicity is the basis for the Roji-the inner tea garden.★

The combined elements of pond, stream, and waterfalls invent the spirit of the place. White sand implies the sea, and granite rocks represent islands in the sea. The rock is the focus of the design. Three pine trees symbolize an impressive stillness in the landscape. By contrast, running water represents the dynamic element of nature. A steep grade enabled the construction of several waterfalls; the largest one is great enough to be called baku, or great fall, and it produces echoes deep in the body. The contrast of stillness and movement is the key element of this design.

This garden further emphasizes that maintaining a balance between opposing forces-stillness and movement-is an important matter for our existence and well-being. Everyday life is full of activities and restlessness. The motion of the powerful waterfall, combined with the presence of the still pines, seems to calm us and clear our restless, worried minds. This is why I named this garden Bakusyou-tei, "The garden of great waterfall and pine trees."

★*Roji is a small garden path setting created for the tea ceremony. Each element is placed according to the rules of tea. The journey through the garden allows the cleansing of oneself before entering the tea house.*

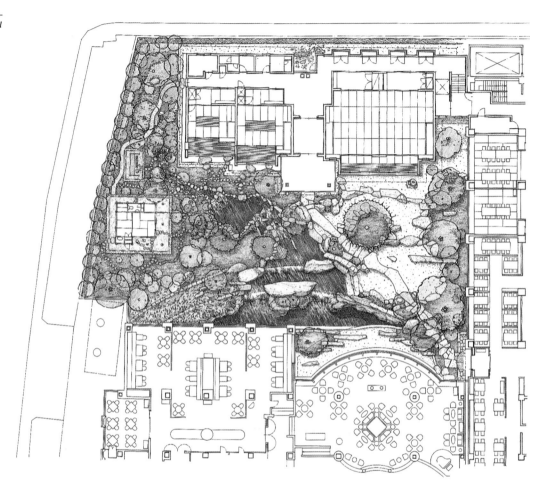

ABOVE RIGHT: *Plan*

RIGHT: *Fashioned stone basin*

LEFT: *Garden overlooked from upper level*

FOLLOWING PAGE: *View to the tea house from the Japanese style annex building*

LEFT: *View from "Nijiriguchi" (miniature entrance to the tea house)*
OPPOSITE PAGE: *Around the tea house*

ABOVE RIGHT: *Image sketch*
RIGHT: *Largest waterfall down to the underground*

ABOVE LEFT: *Sketch*

LEFT: *View from the Japanese restaurant*

FAR LEFT: *View from the garden to the lounge*

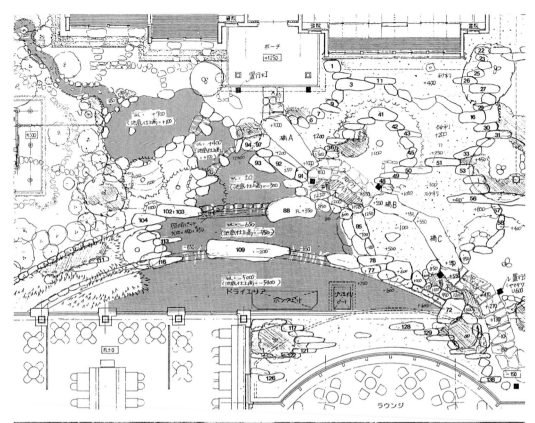

ABOVE RIGHT: *Plan for the layout of rocks*

RIGHT: *View from the lounge*

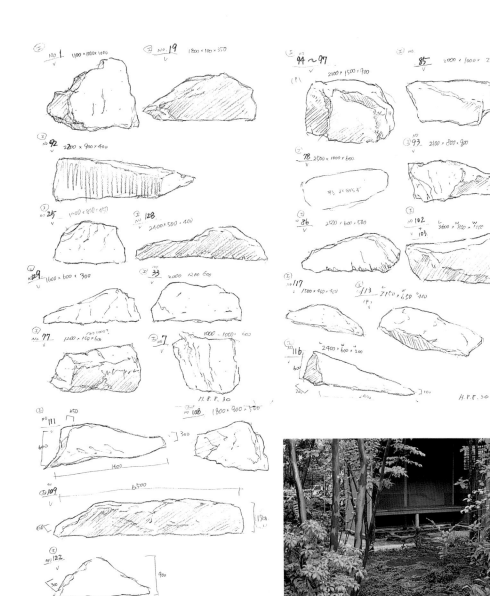

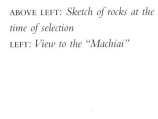

ABOVE LEFT: *Sketch of rocks at the time of selection*

LEFT: *View to the "Machiai"*

HANOURA INFORMATION/ CULTURE CENTER

The Garden of Neither More Nor Less

ABOVE: *Cobble stones and Kousa dogwood*
OPPOSITE PAGE: *Path*

The main feature of this garden is a large body of water surrounded by pine trees. The garden is called, Fuzou-fumetsu to reflect an attitude of facing facts as they are. This attitude is metaphorically expressed in a Chinese legend depicting a carp absorbed in an attempt to climb a waterfall. The carp's virtuous fight moves and reminds us to encounter reality despite earthly desires. The waterfall is called Ryu-mon-baku (the dragon gate of strong waterfall). The process of self-examination or of enduring hardship to gain success is called, To-ryu-mon (to pass through the dragon gate). It is believed that one becomes able to see truths and accept everything undisguised when one has purely confronted difficulties. The real value of a thing does not increase nor decrease according to its contemporary reputation. The spirit of Fuzou-fumetsu (neither more nor less) involves recognizing the significance of being. By concentrated viewing one's spirit will unite with the garden. I believe this is the moment that one feels purified and at absolute peace. The composition of stones in the middle of the garden, called Sanzon-seki, is derived from the Buddhist trinity symbolizing the tranquility of the place.

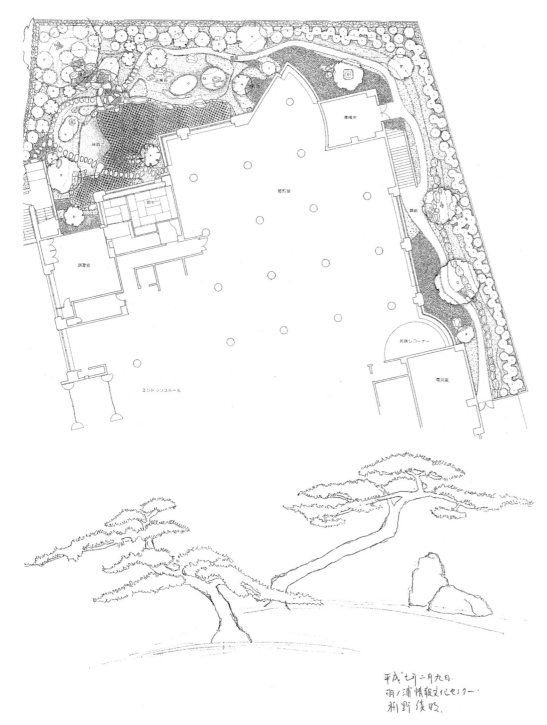

LEFT: *Plan*
BELOW: *Sketch for pine tree*
OPPOSITE PAGE: *Picture window of the library*

平成七年二月九日.
羽ノ浦情報文化センター.
桝野俊明.

ABOVE RIGHT: *Sketch for waterfall and stream*

RIGHT AND FAR RIGHT: *Waterfall*

LEFT: *Waterfall*

LEFT AND OPPOSITE PAGE: *Night view*

LEFT: *Stone lantern and Japanese apricot tree*
OPPOSITE PAGE: *Stepping stones over the pond and water basin*

KAGAWA PREFECTURAL LIBRARY

The Garden where Fresh Winds Blow In and Blow Away

ABOVE: *Chinese Elm and chiseled rocks*
OPPOSITE PAGE: *Chiseled rocks*

Originally this site was used as an airport runway. For many years, the memories, sorrows, and hopes of many people passed through this place. The site was destined to be a powerful place to contemplate the blowing winds and to cultivate a peaceful mind.

An airport-a place of coming and going, of moving into and returning from the heavens-is a perfect site for contemplating the past and dreaming about the future. The goal here was to design the place as a heavenly place, where trees, the sky, and singing birds gently surrounded everything. People who experience the breath of the wind here will never lose their way. This sentiment is represented by its name: Seifuu Kyorai No Niwa (The garden where fresh winds blow in and blow away).

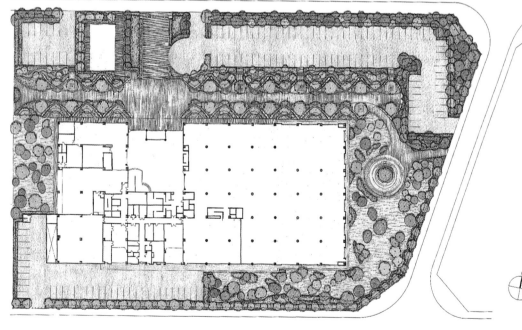

LEFT: *Chinese Elm and stainless circle bench*
BELOW: *Plan*
OPPOSITE PAGE: *Tulip trees and Japanese andromeda planted along site*

RIGHT: *Trees with circular curbing*

LEFT: *Picture window from the library*
BELOW: *Image sketch*

植栽
（アベリア）

植栽
（フッキソウ）

植栽
（アマリリス）

自然石（割肌）

LEFT: *Impressive rocks*
BELOW: *Sketch for designed rocks*
OPPOSITE PAGE: *Placed rocks*

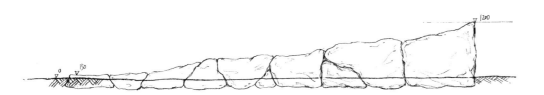

CANADIAN MUSEUM OF CIVILIZATION

The Garden for Harmonious Relationship with Respect

ABOVE: *Stepping stones*
OPPOSITE PAGE: *Waterfall rock arrangement*

This traditional Japanese Zen Garden is located on a public terrace rooftop. It is called, Wakei No Niwa, which, roughly translated, means to understand and respect all cultures-their history, spirit, and people-which leads to cultural harmony. The garden design features an extensive gravel raked garden, a dry "waterfall," and a stone bridge. All materials used in this garden were selected in the hills surrounding the region. The dry waterfall is the focus of the garden and is the symbolic source of Japanese influence.

The garden is oriented toward visitors as they arrive at the place of honor: a special assembly area located in the garden. An axis was formed in a gathering area inside the museum, and it leads to the garden, then extends over the waterfall, across the Ottawa River, and on to the Japanese Embassy. The dry stream wraps around the area, and appears to flow through the windows of the museum's Collections/Administration building, symbolizing the infusion of Japanese culture in Canadian culture.

This garden serves as a museum display as well as being part of the museum's total landscape design. Although it appears complete, this is only the first phase of the project. The next phase of construction will complete the lower level entry to the garden and a planned upper level area above the main garden, which will serve several important functions.

The garden on the upper level is designed to reinforce the connection with the Japanese Embassy across the Ottawa River, and it is a splendid place to view the garden from another perspective. It will be adorned with a natural rock carved into a bench, which will unite the traditional Zen garden with the contemporary expression of Zen.

It is crucial in building such a sparse design to listen to the "conversation" among all the materials-such as the plants and stones-as well as to be aware of the spaces between objects. Both the creator of a Zen garden and the viewer should be "at one" with the garden when they regard it. Our attempt was to help the museum's visitors better understand themselves and their landscape through this garden.

RIGHT: *Plan*

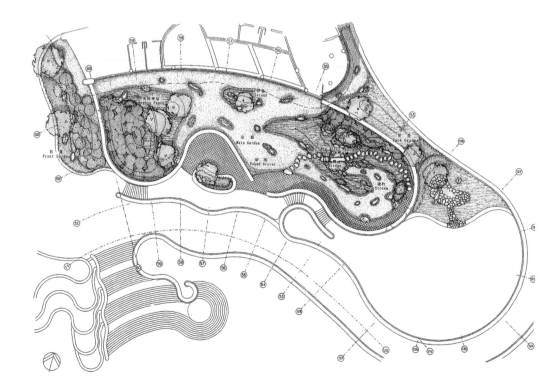

LEFT: *The garden was designed with the building's shape in mind.*

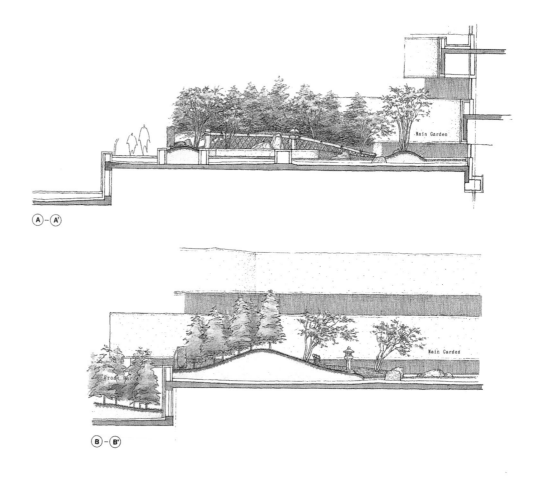

(A)–(A')

(B)–(B')

ABOVE RIGHT: *Section*
RIGHT: *Sketch*

C—C'

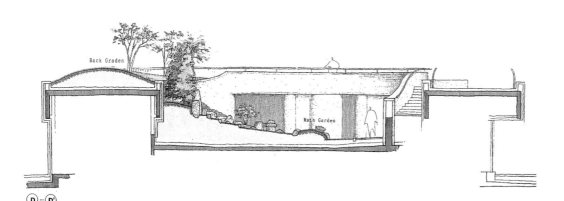

D—D'

ABOVE LEFT: *Section*
LEFT: *Sketch*

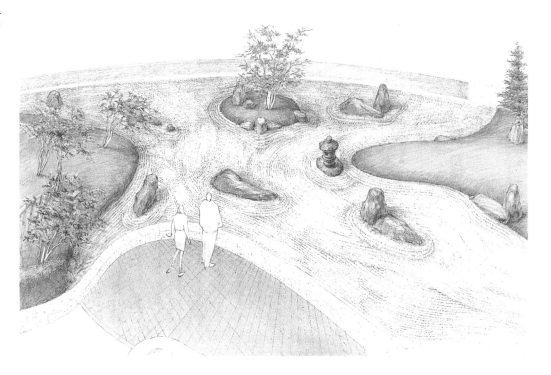

ABOVE RIGHT: *Sketch*
RIGHT: *Sand carved(raked) by Shunmyo*
OPPOSITE PAGE: *Rock arrangement with island in the foreground*

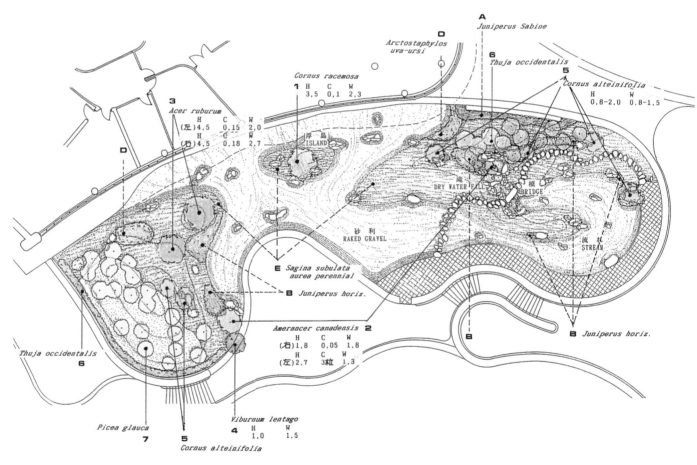

A

D

Juniperus Sabine

Arctostaphylos
uva-ursi

6 Thuja occidentalis

Cornus racemosa

5

Cornus alteinifolia

1 H   C   W
3,5   0,1   2,3

H   W
0,8-2,0   0,8-1,5

3

Acer ruburum

H   C   W
(左)4,5   0,15   2,0
H   C   W
(右)4,5   0,18   2,7

D

浮島
ISLAND

滝
DRY WATER

橋
BRIDGE

砂利
RAKED GRAVEL

流れ
STREAM

E Sagina subulata
aurea perennial

B Juniperus horiz.

Amerancer canadensis **2**

H   C   W
(右)1,8   0,05   1,8
H   C   W
(左)2,7   3粒   1,3

B Juniperus horiz.

Thuja occidentalis

6

B

Picea glauca

7

5

Cornus alteinifolia

Viburnum lentago

4 H   W
1,0   1,5

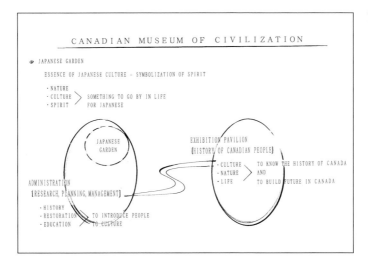

CANADIAN MUSEUM OF CIVILIZATION

⊕ JAPANESE GARDEN

ESSENCE OF JAPANESE CULTURE = SYMBOLIZATION OF SPIRIT

· NATURE
· CULTURE ⟩ SOMETHING TO GO BY IN LIFE
· SPIRIT   FOR JAPANESE

JAPANESE GARDEN

EXHIBITION PAVILION
(HISTORY OF CANADIAN PEOPLE)

· CULTURE TO KNOW THE HISTORY OF CANADA
· NATURE   ⟩ AND
· LIFE   TO BUILD FUTURE IN CANADA

ADMINISTRATION
(RESEARCH, PLANNING, MANAGEMENT)

· HISTORY
· RESTORATION TO INTRODUCE PEOPLE
· EDUCATION   TO CULTURE

ABOVE RIGHT: *Conceptual charts*
RIGHT: *Section*
OPPOSITE PAGE TOP: *Finished water-fall rock arrangement*
OPPOSITE PAGE BOTTOM: *Planting plan*

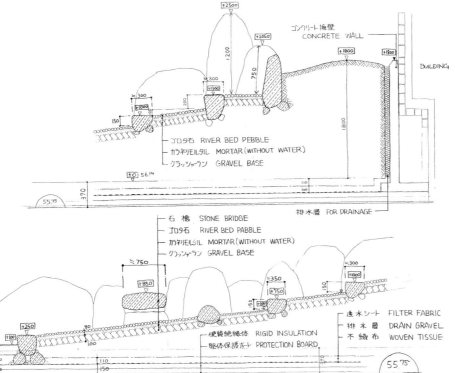

THE UNIVERSITY OF
BRITISH COLUMBIA

Renovation of the Nitobe Garden

ABOVE: *Water flows to the pond*
OPPOSITE PAGE: *Wooden bridge leading onto the island*

This was a major project to restore and renovate gardens that were laid out in 1960, as a memorial to the scholar and educator, Inazo Nitobe, who died while visiting British Columbia. The original plan was designed by Kannosuke Mori. Over the years the gardens had been changed considerably, and the concepts behind its design were no longer discernible. Indeed, it would have been impossible to renovate it at all without removing such impediments as the concrete coating that was sprayed over the original shoreline stonework in 1974 to prevent it from leaking.

The scheme to renovate these gardens was developed after considering what Mori himself would have done had he been alive today. We also investigated the things he wanted to do during the gardens' construction but for some reason was unable to accomplish. We were able to return the original island to the pond, restore the shoreline stonework, and add new beaches. The tea house and garden were also updated and restored. To help shut out the noise of traffic, we constructed a traditional Japanese mud wall around the entire garden. Finally, a pathway and entry gate were constructed to define and locate the gardens.

ABOVE: *Plan*
RIGHT: *Rock arrangement at the ponds edge*
OPPOSITE PAGE: *Another bridge*

PREVIOUS PAGE: *Renovated garden*

ABOVE RIGHT: *Newly constructed main gate*
RIGHT: *Detail of main gate*

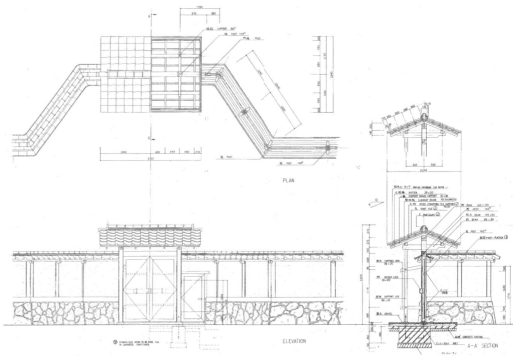

PLAN

ELEVATION

A–A SECTION

LEFT: *Newly constructed "Tsuijibei" wall and stone path*

RIGHT: *The site immediately after renovation work had begun.*

BELOW: *Proposed renovation plan*

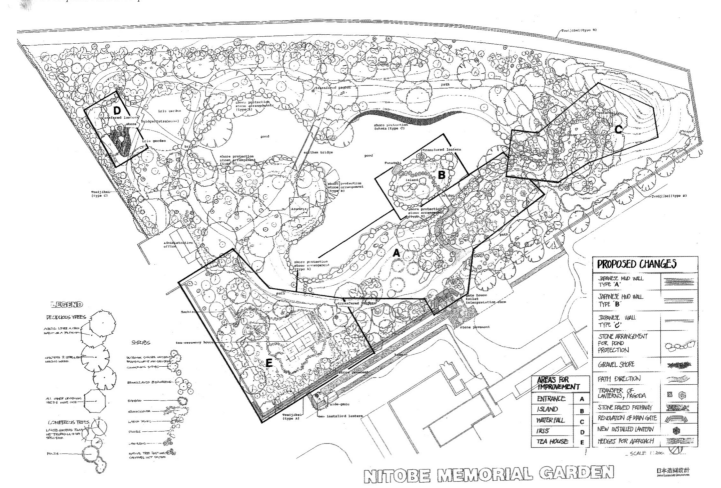

CLOCKWISE FROM TOP RIGHT:
Supervising the placement of rocks at the ponds edge; placing stones for "Nobedan" (path) in the tea garden; supervising the placement of rocks at the ponds edge; supervising the placement of rocks at the ponds edge

ABOVE RIGHT: *Overlooking tea house from "Machiai"*

ABOVE FAR RIGHT: *Renovated tea garden*

RIGHT: *Path to the tea house*

ABOVE LEFT: *Sketch (rock arrangement for waterfall)*
LEFT: *Water cascades into the pond*

NATIONAL RESEARCH INSTITUTE FOR METALS, SCIENCE AND TECHNOLOGY AGENCY

The Plaza of Whiteness Refined by Natural Power

ABOVE: *Group of rocks and pebbled stream*
OPPOSITE PAGE: *Overall view*

The theme of this garden came naturally after a visit to the site. What first struck me was the notion of purity, which is one of the most important and difficult things for people to attain. Scientists working here needed a pure mind to perform. The garden had to be a place where the symbol of purity existed.

In addition, the site called to mind the relationship between man and metal during the American Gold Rush. During that time, thousands of people journeyed into the mountains to pursue their dream. What they found was a dry, inhospitable range of craggy mountains sparsely dotted with scrub trees and grasses. In the valleys there were dry twisting river beds and little water.

The prospectors, therefore, were not only searching for gold; they were also looking for water to relieve their weary bodies. Often they would meet at a place where there was a spring. This was where they found the hope and energy to face another day's toil.

Prospectors worked alone digging and panning for ore. In similar fashion, researchers at this institute also work alone. So despite the differences between a mine and a research laboratory, prospectors and researchers have in common the fact that their work is often a solitary battle. By understanding this similarity, we were able to make the plaza a place where isolated and solitary researchers might be rejuvenated.

What emerged was a dry, chalky landscape scattered with hard, sharp stones. Large stones laid toward the building represent human lives. The stones are washed by rain and polished by the gritty winds, until they are gradually purified and bleached. Man's spirit also is purified by experiencing harsh circumstances.

White is the symbol of purity and of Buddha's heart. In Zen philosophy, the tremendous power of nature revitalizes the weary mind and returns it to its original whiteness. This acetic practice is called byakuren, through which human beings may receive the power of nature and reclaim their pure spirit, in the way that stones are bleached by the sun. The plaza of whiteness refined by natural power is thus a place for the research scientist to rediscover the clarity of his or her goals, direction, and dreams.

RIGHT: *Plan*
OPPOSITE PAGE: *Stone bridge with stepping stones*

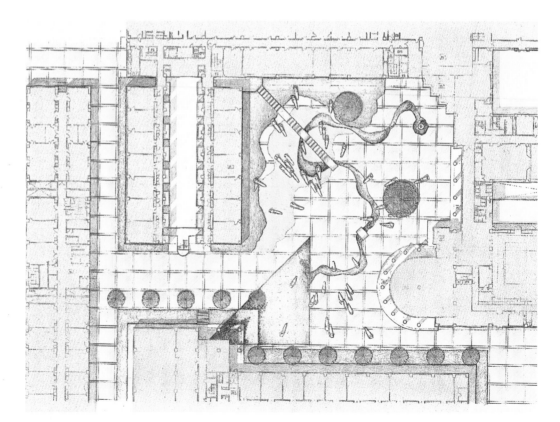

ABOVE RIGHT: *Seen from the entrance hall*

RIGHT: *Perspective*

OPPOSITE PAGE: *Night view*

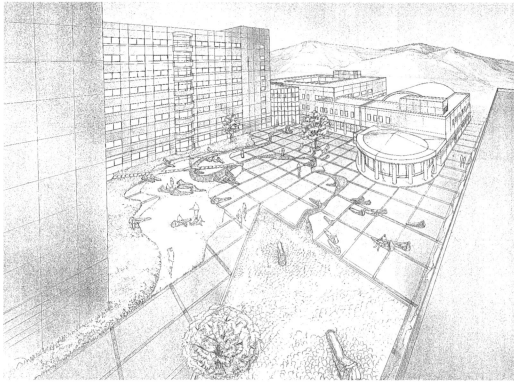

ABOVE RIGHT: *Mist covers the placed rocks*

RIGHT: *The chiseled rocks contrast sharply with the symmetrical paving*

ABOVE LEFT: *Chiseled rock symbolically placed*

LEFT: *Group of rocks placed beside mist*

NIIGATA PREFECTURAL MUSEUM OF MODERN ART

Unity of Earth and Sky

A long-term ambition has been to design a place where people can be absorbed in a magnificent landscape and recognize themselves as part of nature. To produce this, a huge open space was needed. The grounds surrounding the site of the Niigata Prefectural Museum of Modern Art afforded the ideal conditions for such a project. Two-thirds of the building is located underground, so the impression is that it has emerged naturally out of the earth. The Shinano River runs parallel to the site. Standing on the hilltop, with the boundless sky above and the vast, flowing Shinano River below, the view extends towards a peaceful countryside into the horizon. This is a space that enables one to experience the universe.

Tenchi ittai refers to the state of not discriminating among earth, sky, and man. When one realizes that man is a small part of such a vast relationship, we recognize the great power that daily affects our existence. Experiencing tenchi ittai space invokes our thankfulness for our existence. The garden is designed to summon this state into the hearts of the many people who will visit this museum.

Using the Shinano River as a starting point to determine ways in which man can live in harmony with nature, we attempted to develop the design along the two metaphorical axes of time and space.

The museum itself stands at the intersection of the city and nature, which the river represents. Its flow symbolizes not only the passage of time from the past through the present and into the future, but alternatively, its recursive movement once more to the past. In the physical world time moves forward. Within the spiritual world it is possible to retrace one's steps into the past through memories. These two flows of time were considered as we laid out the garden.

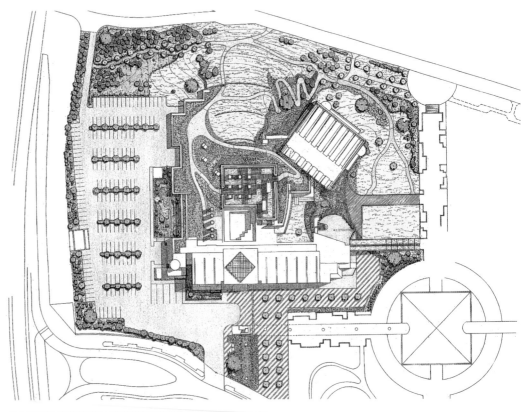

ABOVE RIGHT: *Plan*

RIGHT: *Continuous thread-like white cascade and decorative columns*

ABOVE LEFT: *Front elevation of the museum at night*
LEFT: *Movement of water seen from the lobby*

FOLLOWING PAGES: *Landscaped roof of the museum*

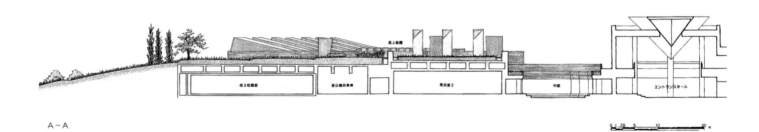

A－A

B－B

C－C

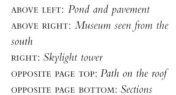

ABOVE LEFT: *Pond and pavement*
ABOVE RIGHT: *Museum seen from the south*
RIGHT: *Skylight tower*
OPPOSITE PAGE TOP: *Path on the roof*
OPPOSITE PAGE BOTTOM: *Sections*

DENENCHOFU PARK CONDOMINIUM

Compatibility

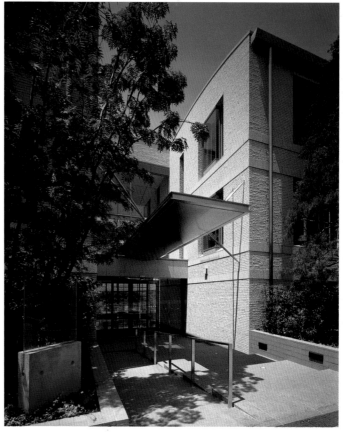

ABOVE: *Modern entrance of the condominium*
OPPOSITE PAGE: *Night view*

This building is located on a hillside covered with rich greenery in one of the most prestigious residential neighborhoods of Tokyo. The western edge of the site was a steep woodland slope. Within the woods a majestic Japanese red pine was dominant. It looked like the master of the land, inheriting its history and governing the site.

The theme for designing the site is yu-wa, or compatibility. This describes the attempt to create a harmonious relationship between the site and its surroundings, the new building the natural topography that surrounds it.

The site's beautiful existing trees are reflected in the four imperatives of the design. The first was to provide lush vegetation along the street front. Second was to preserve as many existing trees as possible. The third was to transplant any trees that lay in the path of construction. The fourth was to ensure that the architectural elements faded into the greenery.

An ornamental wall plays an important role in providing a special experience of the place. It extends from the building and follows the grade. The wall steps to the lower level where a cozy terrace, hidden from view, provides just enough space for an intimate bench. The view from here is dominated by the large Japanese pine.

The building is connected to the site by rocks that cover the surface of the slope around the pine tree. By blending the rough texture and the architectural arrangement, a space was created where a harmonious relationship between man and nature could develop in a severely limited urban space. Today in Tokyo a comforting sitting area under a mature tree's canopy is indeed a rarity. The condominium provides an experience seldom enjoyed in today's Tokyo.

RIGHT: *Plan*

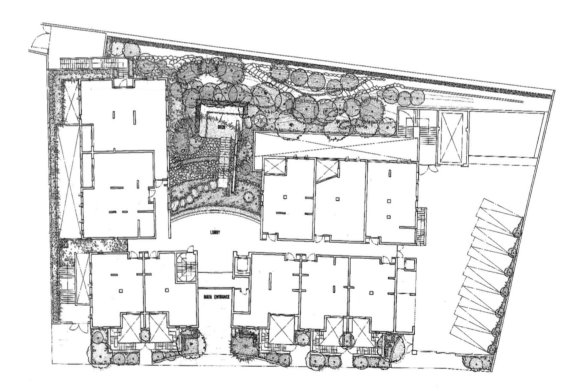

LEFT: *Existing big red pine tree creating the shade to the steps*

ABOVE: *Sketch for terrace*
RIGHT: *Ornamental wall, steps, and terrace*

LEFT: *Utilizing existing stepping stones*

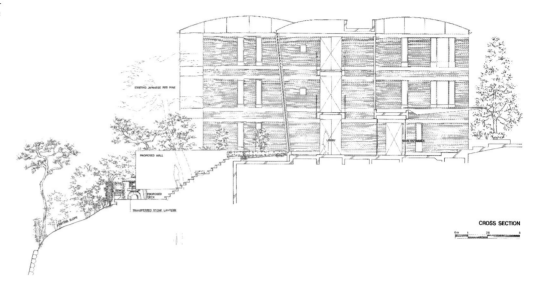

CROSS SECTION

ABOVE RIGHT: *Section*
RIGHT: *Planting plan for transferred and preserved trees*

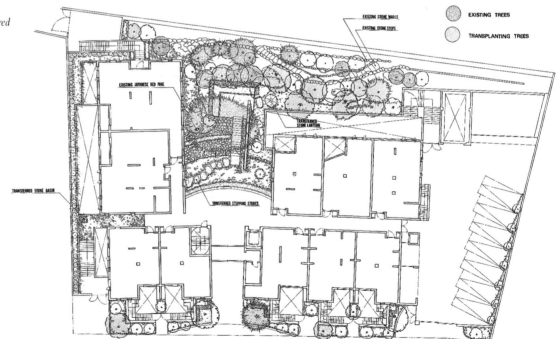

EXISTING STONE WALLS

EXISTING STONE STEPS

EXISTING TREES

TRANSPLANTING TREES

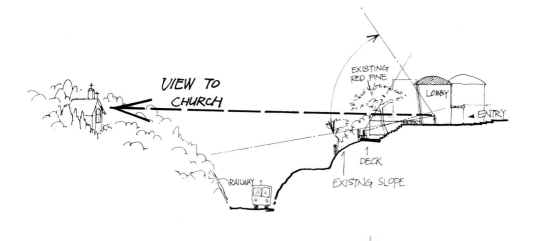

VIEW TO CHURCH

EXISTING RED PINE

LOBBY

ENTRY

DECK

EXISTING SLOPE

RAILWAY

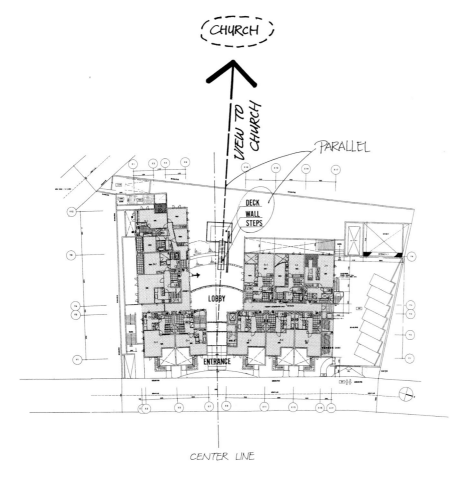

CHURCH

VIEW TO CHURCH

PARALLEL

DECK WALL STEPS

LOBBY

ENTRANCE

CENTER LINE

LEFT: *Plan indicating an axis*

LETHAM GRANGE HOTEL AND GOLF COURSE

Stones of Good Fortune

ABOVE: *Placed rock in one with nature*
OPPOSITE PAGE: *Placed rocks*

In this project, I "blow spirits" into the stones that have slept deep within the bowels of the earth for millennia. These stones, excavated from a quarry in Aberdeen, Scotland, were destined to be crushed for road fill. Yet, for the sixty-six stones selected from the huge quarry, my visit changed their destiny. When I create a stone composition, I first gaze into the "spirit" of each stone to learn and memorize its character. This is the beginning of many conversations I hold with the stones. Then I set them with great care to liberate their characteristics (which I call ishi gokoro, or "the heart of the stone") as much as possible.

The stones are truly happy to cooperate with me in my work. Especially the stones used in this project, for now they rest in the most beautiful areas on the golf course, perhaps for eternity. When visitors see or touch the stones, they will witness their lives in the long history and good fortune of the stones. Providing an opportunity for people to pursue the spirit of Zen and to think about their own life is one of my life's great pleasures.

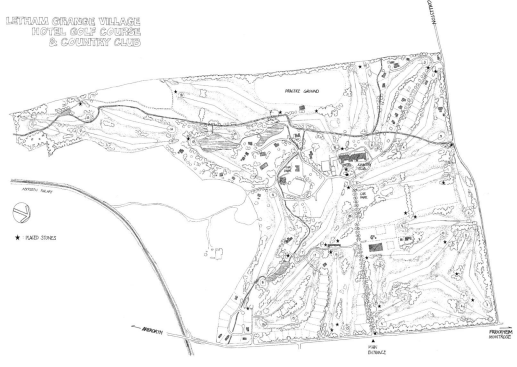

LETHAM GRANGE VILLAGE
HOTEL GOLF COURSE
& COUNTRY CLUB

PRACTICE GROUND

ABERDEEN RAILWAY

★ = PLACED STONES

ARBROATH

CAR PARK

HOTEL

COUNTRY CLUB

CAR PARK

MAIN ENTRANCE

COLLISTON

FRIOCKHEIM
MONTROSE

ABOVE: *Plan*
LEFT: *Symbolically placed rock*
OPPOSITE PAGE: *Symbolically placed rock*

ABOVE RIGHT: *Placed rocks in front of the hotel*

RIGHT: *Supervising placement of rocks*

NO2 + NO4. + NO7   IN FRONT OF HOTEL

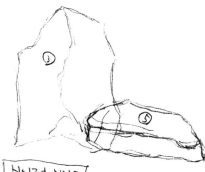

NO3 + NO5   ENTRANCE

NO12+ NO10

LEFT: *Sketch for rocks*
FAR LEFT: *Quarry rocks at Aberdeen*

SELECTED GARDENS

HOTEL KOHJIMACHI KAIKAN
Client: Ministry of Home Affairs
Date of Completion: March 1998
Location: 2-4-3 Hirakawa-cho Chiyoda-ku Tokyo
Architect: Sato Sougou Keikaku
Contractor: Takenaka Corporation
Landscape Contractor: Hibiya Amenis (cooperated with
  Shinichi Sano, Uetoh Zoen)
Stone Works: Masatoshi Izumi
Photo Credit: Minao Tabata (Pages 12-17, 20-21)
  Shunmyo Masuno (Page 19)

IMABARI KOKUSAI HOTEL
Client: Imabari Shipbuilding Co.,Ltd.
Date of Completion: October 1996
Location: 2-3-4 Asahi-machi Imabari city Ehime
Architect: Kanko Kikaku Sekkeisha + Naniwa Sekkei
Contractor: Shimizu Corporation
Landscape Contractor: Shinichi Sano, Uetoh Zoen and
  Masatoshi Izumi (stone work)
Photo Credit: Minao Tabata (Pages 22-33)

HANOURA INFORMATION/CULTURE CENTER
Client: Hanoura town
Date of Completion: June 1995
Location: Hanoura Nakagun, Tokushima
Architect: Ishimoto Architectural & Engineering Firm. Inc.
Contractor: Oobayashi Corporation
Landscape Contractor: Oobayashi Corporation in
cooperation with Matsuyama Ryokuchi Kensetsu
Photo Credit: Haruo Hirota (Pages 34-43)

KAGAWA PREFECTURAL LIBRARY
Client: Kagawa Prefecture
Date of Completion: December 1993
Location: Hayashi-cho Takamatsu city
Architect: Ishimoto Architectural & Engineering Firm. Inc.
Contractor: Kajima Corporation

Landscape Contractor: Kajima Corporation in cooperation with Masatoshi Izumi (stone works) and five landscape contractors
Photo Credit: Haruo Hirota (Pages 44-51)

CANADIAN MUSEUM OF CIVILIZATION
Client: Canadian Museum of Civilization
Date of Completion: May 1995
Location: 100 Laurier Street Hull, Quebec, Canada
Architect: Douglas Cardinal
Local Consultant: Don Vaughn Ltd.
Landscape Contractor: Shinichi Sano, Uetoh Zoen, and a Canadian local contractor
Photo Credit: Shunmyo Masuno (Pages 52-60)

RENOVATION OF NITOBE GARDEN
Client: The University Of British Columbia
Date of Completion: August 1993
Location: Southwest Marine Drive Vancouver Canada
Local Consultant: Don Vaughn Ltd.
Landscape Contractor: Shinichi Sano, Uetoh Zoen + Double V Construction Ltd. (Canada)
Photo Credit: Haruo Hirota (Pages 62-69, 72-73)
    Shunmyo Masuno (Pages 70-71)

PLAZA, NATIONAL RESEARCH INSTITUTE FOR METALS, SCIENCE AND TECHNOLOGY AGENCY
Client: Metals, Science and Technology Agency
Date of Completion: December 1993
Location: 1-2 Sengen Tsukuba city, Ibaragi
Architect: Nihon Sekkei Inc. + RIA
Contractor: Hazama Corporation
Landscape Contractor: Hazama Corporation in cooperation with Masatoshi Izumi (stone works) and Hibiya Amenis
Photo Credit: Haruo Hirota (Pages 74-81)

NIIGATA PREFECTURAL MUSEUM OF MODERN ART
Client: Niigata Prefecture
Date of Completion: May 1993
Location: Nagaoka city, Niigata
Architect: Nihon Sekkei Inc.
Contractor: Taisei Corporation
Landscape Contractor: Taisei Corporation in cooperation with 11 landscape contractors
Photo Credit: Haruo Hirota (Pages 82-89)

DENENCHOFU PARK CONDOMINIUM
Client: Mitsui Real Estate Co.
Date of Completion: March 1998
Location: 2-26-27 Denenchoufu Oota, Tokyo
Architect: Tokyo Design Center / Genzaburoh Yamanaka
Contractor: Takenaka Corporation
Landscape Contractor: Mitsui Greentech
Photo Credit: Tokyo Design Center (Pages 90-95)

LETHAM GRANGE HOTEL & GOLF COURSE
Client: Letham Grange Hotel & Golf Course
Date of Completion: December 1996
Location: Colliston Angus Scotland
Landscape Contractor: Shinichi Sano (Uetoh Zoen)
Photo Credit: Shunmyo Masuno (Pages 98-103)

Additional Photo credits:
Ben Simmons (Pages 7, 9, 10-11)
Shunmyo Masuno (Page 8)

FIRM PROFILE

Shunmyo Masuno studied in the Agricultural Faculty of Tamagawa University in Tokyo. After graduating in 1975, he became a pupil of Katsuo Saito, for whom he had worked while he was still at the University. In 1979 he entered Daihonzan-Soji-ji Temple where he underwent ascetic training to become a priest. He established Japan Landscape Consultants in 1982 and became assistant resident priest at Kenkoh-ji temple in 1985. He has lectured at Cornell University, Toronto University, and Harvard University's Graduate School of Design. He is the recipient of several design awards including the Award of Merit from the University of British Columbia (1994), National Merit Award from the Canadian Society of Landscape Architects (1995), National Grand Prize from the Japanese Institute of Landscape Architecture (1997), the Encouragement Prize of Culture from Yokohama City (1997), and the Annual Award (to encourage new talent in fine arts) from the Japan Ministry of Education (1999).

Other works by Shunmyo Masuno include the Canadian Embassy in Tokyo, the new campus of Tokyo Metropolitan University, Kyoto Reception Hall, and the Takamatsu City crematory. He has served as a professor at Tama Art University and an adjunct professor at the University of British Columbia.

He continues to head Japan Landscape Consultants and to fulfill his duties as assistant priest at Kenkoh-ji Temple.